TSUNAMIS

Louise and Richard Spilsbury

WAYLAND

First published in 2007 by Wayland

Copyright © Wayland 2007

Wayland,
Hachette Children's Books
338 Euston Road,
London NW1 3BH

Wayland Australia
Level 17/207 Kent Street
Sydney, NSW 2000

Editor: Susie Brooks
Managing Editor: Rasha Elsaeed
Designer: Tim Mayer, MayerMedia
Picture Researcher: Shelley Noronha

British Library Cataloguing in Publication Data
Spilsbury, Louise
    Tsunamis. - (Natural Disasters)
    1. Tsunamis - Juvenile literature
    I. Title II. Spilsbury, Richard, 1963-
    551.4'637

ISBN 9780750250467

Wayland is a division of Hachette Children's Books, an Hachette Livre UK company.

Photo credits: Cover, 4 ©Jeremy Horner/Corbis; 1, 36 ©Teru Kuwayama/Corbis; Bckgd 3-48 ©Guy Gelfenbaum/USGS; Bckgd (panels) 4-45 ©Bruce Jaffe/USGS; 5 ©Kieran Doherty/Reuters/Corbis; 6, 16-17 ©National Geophysical Data Center/ NOAA; 7, 19, 23, 25, 26, 31 ©Reuters/Corbis; 9 ©State Palace/epa/Corbis; 10-11 ©South American Pictures/Robert Francis/NAB00001s2; 12, 13, 15 ©Keith Dannemiller/Corbis; 14 ©Harry Yeh, University of Washington; 18 ©Sankei Shimbun/Corbis Sygma; 20-21 ©Eriko Sugita/Reuters/ Corbis; 24 ©Rick Rycroft/AP/PA Photos; 27 ©Michael John/University of Papua New Guinea; 28, 30 ©Bruce Jaffe/USGS; 32-33 ©South American Pictures /Tony Morrison/PDF0057s2; 34-35 ©Digital Globe/ZUMA/ Corbis; 37 ©Chaiwat Subprasom/Reuters/Corbis; 38 ©Babu/ Reuters/Corbis; 39 ©Mike Alquinto/epa/Corbis; 40 ©James Robert Fuller/-Corbis; 41 ©Pallava Bagla/Corbis; 42-43 ©AFP/ Getty Images; 44 ©BPPT/Handout/Reuters/Corbis; 45 ©Narong Sangnak/epa/Corbis

CONTENTS

What is a tsunami?

A tsunami is a huge, powerful and often destructive wave. The wave usually begins as barely a ripple out in deep ocean water, but it can reach immense size by the time it hits a coastline. The name tsunami comes from the Japanese for 'harbour wave'. It was first used by fishermen who returned to shore to find their harbour villages devastated by these mysterious surges of water, which they had not seen out at sea. Throughout history tsunamis have swept over coasts around the world, taking hundreds of thousands of lives.

Mighty waves

Some people call tsunamis tidal waves, but tsunamis are not caused by changing tides and they do not form like ordinary waves. Most ordinary waves are caused by the force of winds blowing against the surface of the ocean. They break and curl over when they come ashore, which is when surfers ride them. Tsunamis can be very long and deep and they do not break like ordinary waves. They travel like dark, fast-moving walls of water, up to tens of metres tall and several kilometres wide.

A large tsunami can hurl thousands of tonnes of water on to land at once, so it is hardly surprising that tsunamis can cause severe damage to any coastal region. They have the power to sweep away everything in their path, from people, trees and houses to roads, bridges and boats. Worst of all, one wave is usually followed by others, which may be even deadlier.

FAST AND FURIOUS

Some of the biggest tsunamis in the world can be 40 metres higher than the average sea level. In deep water, tsunamis can race along at incredible speeds of up to 800 kph!

Tsunamis move and grow quickly. People say that if you can see a tsunami wave from the shore, then it may be too late to outrun it. This one is striking the coast of Thailand.

Giant tsunamis are the most destructive waves on Earth. This is what was left of a village on the eastern coast of Sri Lanka after a major tsunami struck in January 2005.

When a tsunami comes

One of the classic signs that a tsunami is coming is when the sea suddenly retreats dramatically from a beach or shore. The water is literally sucked back, exposing large areas of sand or rock that are not usually uncovered even at low tide. Then comes a strong wind, which is pushed forwards by the force of the approaching tsunami. After this, a series of tsunami waves, called a wave train, smacks into the shore and may continue hitting the land for hours afterwards.

EYEWITNESS

❝ I looked up and saw a huge wall of dirty water. Palm trees 11 metres tall were covered by water… just as the wave struck our house. It felt like we'd been hit by a train. The wave picked up the house, and we floated away… All I could see past my hanging clothes were waves and dead fish. ❞

Mieko "Miki" Browne, who was caught up in a tsunami in Hawaii in April 1940

How tsunamis form

Tsunamis are caused by a sudden shift at the surface of an expanse of water. Most are triggered by underwater earthquakes. The sudden jerking movement caused by an earthquake creates waves at the surface. Tsunami waves usually happen in oceans, but they can also occur in lakes, reservoirs or inland seas.

Underwater earthquakes

Underwater earthquakes occur in the same way as earthquakes on land. The centre of the Earth is so hot that the rock there is molten, or liquid. The cooler outer layer of rock that makes up the surface of the planet is called the crust. As the crust cooled and hardened long ago, it cracked into giant pieces, called tectonic plates. The plates are up to 100 kilometres thick and they float on top of the molten rock, moving very slowly. Sometimes the plate boundaries pull apart or grind past each other, or one plate dips under another. When these actions cause a sudden jolt they can create an earthquake.

Underwater earthquakes may not be felt on land, so the tsunamis they produce often hit coastlines unexpectedly. These movie stills show how a tsunami wave triggered by an earthquake in Japan raced in and swept a car from the shore.

Other causes of tsunamis

There are other events that can cause vast amounts of water to move suddenly. Many tsunamis are brought on by underwater landslides, or landslides at the coast that cause rock or ice to fall into the water. When a large chunk of rock hits the surface of the sea and sinks, water sucked down on either side of the rock collides in the middle and the impact sends enormous waves radiating out. Some landslides are the result of earthquakes, but others may be triggered by heavy rainfall. In 1994 a new wharf being built at Skagway, Alaska was suddenly washed off land by storms, causing an underwater landslide that created tsunami waves 11 metres high.

Some tsunamis are caused by underwater volcanoes that explode through the Earth's crust and shake the sea. In 1883, the Krakatau volcano exploded and created waves 40 metres high that demolished parts of Indonesia, killing more than 36,000 people.

TSUNAMIS FROM SPACE!

Tsunamis have been caused by asteroid impact. When the Eltanin asteroid hit Earth 2.5 million years ago, the tsunami that followed spread across the entire Pacific and Atlantic oceans in just one day and swamped the coasts of South America and Antarctica.

An explosion of volcanic dust and steam blasts out of the Pacific Ocean. Underwater eruptions like this sometimes cause tsunamis.

Slowing and growing

As tsunami waves travel from the deep ocean to the shore, they change. In deep water tsunami waves move very fast, but at this point they are less than a few metres high so they are not dangerous. When they reach shallower waters near a shore, the front of the waves starts to slow down and water piles up behind. Now the tsunami waves increase in height, becoming tall and dangerous walls of water that can strike the land with the impact of solid concrete.

Where tsunamis happen

Four out of every five tsunamis happen in the Pacific Ocean, along the boundary of a vast tectonic plate. The remaining fifth occur anywhere where earthquakes or landslides trigger a large displacement (movement) of water. In the past tsunamis have battered places such as coastal regions of Canada, at the edge of the Atlantic Ocean, and Turkey and Greece by the Mediterranean Sea.

Ring of Fire

Tsunamis occur frequently in the Pacific Ocean because the area lies over the Pacific plate, one of Earth's main tectonic plates. Many earthquakes and volcanoes occur along the edges of this plate, where it comes into contact with other sections of the Earth's crust. This is such an active zone for earthquakes and volcanic eruptions that it is known as the 'Ring of Fire'. Any coastal area along the Ring of Fire, or in any part of the Pacific region, is at risk of being hit by tsunamis.

The purple shading on this map shows the areas most at risk from tsunamis. The black lines represent the tectonic plate boundaries, where most of the earthquakes and volcanic eruptions that trigger tsunamis occur.

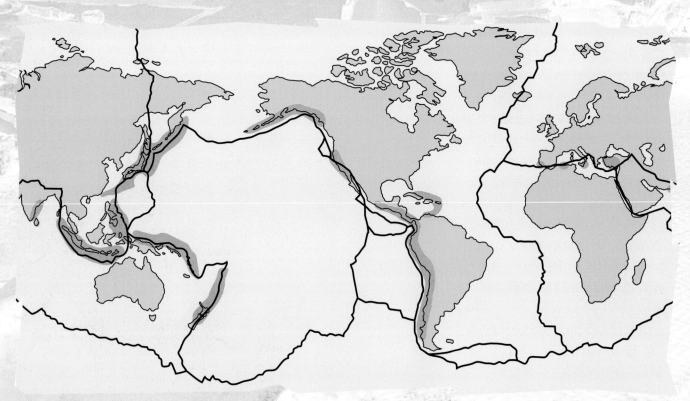

Topography

The other thing that affects where tsunamis happen and how large they become is the topography, or shape, of the land. For example, flat, low-lying coasts and islands are badly affected by tsunamis because even small waves can travel fast and far over land like this, without steep slopes or hills to slow them down or block their path. The distance a tsunami travels inland is called the inundation zone.

The effect of a tsunami can also be increased by headlands, curved bays or fjords. A fjord is a river valley that is very narrow with high sides. When waves wash into a landform like this, or a curved bay, they are squashed into a confined space and can become very tall. The highest tsunami ever recorded happened in Lituya Bay on the southern coast of Alaska in 1958. A landslide at one end of the bay caused a tsunami that grew to over 500 metres tall in the narrow fjord. It tore the trees from the fjord sides, but killed only two people who were on a boat in the bay. When tsunami waves hit a headland (a narrow wedge of rock sticking out from a coast) they can wrap around it so that water floods on to the shore from both sides of the headland.

Meulaboh in Sumatra suffered severe damage from the December 2004 Pacific Ocean tsunami because of its topography. High waves quickly covered the low-lying coastline in this region.

DROWNED ISLAND

Some people believe that an ancient and mysterious island city called Atlantis was lost to the sea many thousands of years ago after a tsunami in the Atlantic Ocean. The Ancient Greek philosopher, Plato wrote: 'There occurred violent earthquakes and floods... the island of Atlantis disappeared in the depths of the sea.'

NICARAGUA, 1992

In the early evening of 2 September 1992, an earthquake shook the bed of the Pacific Ocean about 120 kilometres off the coast of Nicaragua, Central America. Few people on shore were aware that a quake had happened. The first sign that something was wrong was when the seawater quickly receded, as if a plug had been pulled out at the bottom of the ocean. Then a towering wall of water suddenly rushed forward. The tsunami waves killed 170 people and caused widespread devastation.

The impact

The first wave that smashed into the Nicaraguan coast at 6.36 pm, 20 minutes after the earthquake, was not the biggest. It was closely followed by two more destructive waves that were 10 metres high in some places. This wave train struck along a 220-kilometre stretch of the Nicaraguan coastline.

No one on land was prepared for the impact. The tsunami took the people on the shore by complete surprise because the earthquake did not make the earth shake and there were no rumbling sounds. These signs might have warned people that an earthquake had happened and that they should make for higher ground in case a tsunami followed.

COASTAL POPULATION

Nicaragua's Pacific coast is made up of low-lying land in the west of the country. Most of Nicaragua's population lives in this region and over a quarter lives in and around Managua, the capital city. In 1992, Nicaragua was less economically developed than it is today and most of its inhabitants were relatively poor. Many of the people in the coastal region worked as fishermen and lived by the sea in flimsy huts.

San Juan del Sur was a peaceful fishing village on the coast of southern Nicaragua before it was suddenly attacked by the devastating tsunami.

Steady but deadly

The earthquake on 2 September was rated at 7.0 on the Richter scale, a measure that is not usually powerful enough to create dramatic tsunami waves. The problem was that this was a slow earthquake. Although there was a large displacement, or drop, between the tectonic plates, the earthquake created only a mild shaking of the ground. However, this energy was released over about 100 seconds, which is a relatively long time for earthquakes. When its slow release of energy was accounted for, scientists increased the earthquake's rating to 7.6 on the Richter scale.

RICHTER SCALE

The Richter scale is a system for measuring the size of an earthquake. The higher the number on the scale, the more powerful the earthquake is. The weakest earthquakes are rated 1 and the maximum strength on the scale is 10. It usually takes an earthquake with a magnitude (strength) of more than 7.5 to produce a destructive tsunami.

TSUNAMI COSTS

- 170 people killed
- 40,000 people affected
- 13,000 people left homeless
- Cost of damage: US$25 million

A man sits among the ruins of his village, El Transito. The Nicaraguan tsunami left thousands of people without homes or other shelter.

Deaths and damage

As the tsunami hit the coast of Nicaragua, waves swept away many of the homes, restaurants and bars that lined the beaches, as well as the people who had been dining and drinking in them and the cars parked outside. In some places the waves flooded up to 400 metres inland, leaving a path of destruction in their wake. Many people drowned as they struggled but failed to keep their heads above water when dragged out of their depth by the force of the waves. Other casualties were the result of people being hit by rocks that were picked up and carried inland by the water, or by debris from damaged buildings that was snapped off by the waves and then tossed about. Some people were hit by vehicles that were hurled around by the tsunami's power.

After the event it was calculated that the tsunami had affected 40,000 people in 27 different communities and left 13,000 people homeless. It also cost Nicaragua, already a poor country, a huge amount of money, with losses estimated at US$25 million. The tsunami destroyed almost all of Nicaragua's fishing fleet, leaving vast numbers of people without work. Many structures were damaged, including freshwater wells that were ruined when they were flooded with salty seawater.

Many people who made their living from the sea were left without employment when the tsunami destroyed their boats.

Help at hand

Local and international aid teams were quick to arrive. Members of the Nicaraguan army rescued survivors and helped to carry the wounded to hospitals. People from abroad donated money for relief workers to buy supplies direct from Nicaragua, such as temporary shelters, blankets, rolls of plastic sheeting to cover belongings or create makeshift tents, drinking water, fuel, and medicines such as penicillin. Items such as radios and mobile phones were also needed because communication systems were damaged and search-and-rescue team workers needed to be able to contact each other. People experienced in disaster relief situations were also sent from agencies such as the Red Cross to help.

EYEWITNESS

❝ Suddenly the boat whipped around very, very fast. It was dark. We had no idea what had happened. We found ourselves staring into a hill of water rushing toward the shore. I could see the lights of the city through the water. And then the swell hit, and the lights went out, and we could hear people screaming. ❞

Chris Terry, who was aboard his fishing boat in San Juan del Sur harbour when the tsunami struck

Varying power

Damage from tsunamis can seem cruelly random. While one place on a coast can be devastated, another nearby may escape with much less harm. In 1992, the damage was terrible in a part of the coast called El Transito, but nearby Playa Hermosa escaped with much less destruction. The reason for this was that just off El Transito there is a 20-metre gap in the coral reef that stretches along the front of most of the central coast of Nicaragua. El Transito had become a busy fishing village because of the gap in the reef, which allows boats to navigate in and out easily. However, when the tsunami hit, the waves were forced through the gap right into El Transito. Some people managed to escape before the second and third waves hit the shore, having survived the first of the waves which was the smallest of the three.

Differences in damage

Differences in the amount of damage also came about because of the different types of building construction. Many fishermen and their families lived in wooden huts with palm-leaf roofs, and these suffered much more destruction than the sturdy concrete tourist hotels found along some parts of the coast. The fact that the tsunami arrived in the early evening made matters worse. In some places inland, the water rose by 1-1.5 metres and caused few casualties. However, the same water level in some fishing villages drowned many people, especially children, because they were asleep on the floors of fishermen's huts on the beach when the devastating waves came crashing in.

Some buildings remained intact after the tsunami. The weak hut on the left of this photograph survived because the waves flowed between the stilts it is built on. The house on the right has a sturdier structure that largely withstood the force of the water.

A man collects roof tiles from the tsunami debris. Many building materials were salvaged from the rubble in Nicaragua so that they could be used in new constructions.

SILENT KILLER

An estimated 5-10 per cent of tsunami-causing earthquakes are of the kind experienced in Nicaragua – so-called silent earthquakes. These earthquakes release their energy more slowly than the usual sudden lurch, so their true power can easily be underestimated. Experts believe these silent earthquakes may have been responsible for some of the most damaging tsunamis in history, such as one in Japan in 1896.

Lessons learned

The tsunami in Nicaragua was a stark reminder to scientists that large tsunamis can be caused by slow, silent earthquakes. The earthquake here had been underestimated because underwater instruments that measure the shaking of the ground had not picked up most of the longer waves of movement from the quake. Scientists realized that seismometers that can pick up long, slow waves of earthquake activity should be linked to warning systems to forecast tsunami danger in the future.

Warning systems

Something else that became clear after the 1992 tsunami was that communication networks in the area were not good, and that there was no efficient warning system in place to tell people to evacuate quickly. By 1998, there were new seismic stations along the coast that could detect earthquakes and relay messages to a headquarters within minutes. From the headquarters, messages can now be given out over radios to alert even remote fishing villages if a tsunami is approaching.

JAPAN, 1993

At 10.17 pm on 12 July 1993, an underwater earthquake measuring 7.8 on the Richter scale occurred in the Sea of Japan. Its epicentre (starting point) was 15-30 kilometres west of the Japanese islands of Okushiri and Hokkaido. The trembling of the sea bed displaced a large amount of water and created a tsunami that travelled at twice the speed of Japan's fastest train towards the land. Minutes later, the waves engulfed the Okushiri coastline and the central west coast of Hokkaido. It was one of the largest and most devastating tsunamis in Japan's history.

DANGER ZONE

Japan lies in the Pacific Ocean, to the east of China, Russia and Korea. It is made up of more than 3,000 islands, all formed by volcanic activity, and is situated above a region where there is a lot of tectonic plate movement. This means that Japan experiences up to 5,000 earthquakes a year, and therefore is vulnerable to tsunamis too. Another reason why tsunamis are a major threat in Japan is that islands are naturally surrounded on all sides by water. So it is hardly surprising that the word tsunami is Japanese.

Waves of terror

When the tsunami waves reached the shore and crashed into the islands they were over 20 metres high. People tried to outrun the waves, but the depth of the tsunami and the speed at which it moved made this impossible. The sound of the waves was horrific as they swept up buildings, vehicles, docked vessels and other heavy objects at coastal storage areas.

The force and speed of the water was immense. For example, a 70-metre long steel barge was picked up and flung 75 metres from the harbour. Heavy or sharp objects in the moving water were transformed into lethal battering rams that pounded, damaged and destroyed anything in their path. The noise of the water mixed with terrible metallic crashing sounds.

Main impact zone

The area hit by the highest waves was on the tiny island of Okushiri, where a small, V-shaped valley opened into the sea. When the tsunami rushed into the valley, it was funnelled into a tight space and rose higher. Water hitting the end of the valley reached a terrifying 32 metres above sea level. It equalled about the height and force of a moving eight-storey office block.

This clock, found among the debris at Aonae, southern Okushiri, stopped after being damaged by water from the 1993 tsunami. It shows that the waves hit the area less than 15 minutes after the earthquake.

DISASTER DAYS

12 JULY 1993
10.17 pm Earthquake of magnitude 7.8 on the Richter scale strikes off the coasts of Hokkaido and Okushiri islands.

10.20 pm First tsunami wave crashes on to the western shore of Okushiri.

10.22 pm Sapporo District Meteorological Observatory issues a tsunami warning.

10.27 pm Second large tsunami wave hits Okushiri from the east, carrying boats into the main town.

13 JULY
Government gives survivors shelter and provides food in school gymnasiums. Injured people are flown to hospital in Hokkaido City.

17 JULY
Temporary prefabricated emergency cottages are erected on high ground for survivors. People return to work, including fishermen.

JULY 1998
The Japanese government has spent millions of dollars on coastal improvements such as new sea walls to protect Okushiri. It has also paid for extensive rebuilding of roads, property and public buildings damaged by the 1993 disaster. The costs are huge because new structures are designed and made to survive tsunamis that may come in the future.

JAPAN, 1993

Smoke billows from the widespread fires in Aonae after the tsunami.

Looking at losses

The worst damage from the tsunami occurred on the south-western shores of Hokkaido and on Okushiri Island. Okushiri is a small fishing and holiday resort island with many ships, homes and businesses. Most of the homes on Okushiri were made with wooden frames and the waves simply swept these away. A trail of wood, roofing materials and personal belongings from inside the houses was left scattered over a massive area. In many places only the concrete foundations of the houses remained. Many small and large fishing boats had been dropped among the wreckages of towns and villages. The tsunami waves had also stripped plants and grasses from hillsides.

Fire!

Fires often occur after a tsunami. The destructive force of tsunami waves breaks gas lines, knocks over fuel containers and snaps electrical cables, causing dangerous sparks and flames. Numerous blazes broke out following the tsunami in Aonae, a village on the southern tip of Okushiri. Spilled gases such as propane and kerosene (used for heating) fuelled fires that spread quickly because they were fanned by strong winds. Access for fire engines was blocked by debris from the tsunami, so the fires continued to burn fiercely through the night, eventually destroying 340 homes and killing two people. The damage was so great that it took almost five years to rebuild or replace the homes that either partially or totally collapsed in the flames.

AONAE VILLAGE

The village of Aonae on Okushiri was surrounded by sea on three sides. In just an hour, this community was devastated by 13 tsunami waves, each over 2 metres high, that came from different directions and included some that had rebounded off Hokkaido.

People attempt to rescue belongings from the jumble of debris that was once the thriving tourist centre of Aonae.

A wave's progress

Tsunamis spread out from their source in all directions, rather like the ripples that form when a pebble falls into a pond. This means that their effects can be far-reaching. The tsunamis that spread away from the earthquake in Japan in 1993 struck the south-eastern coast of Russia within 30 minutes, where waves ranging from 1-4 metres climbed the shore. After 90 minutes, the tsunami reached the coast of South Korea, which experienced waves of 1-2 metres. Although these places did not suffer anything like the devastation that occurred on Okushiri or Hokkaido, many of their local fishing boats were damaged or lost.

TSUNAMI COSTS

- 239 people killed
- 437 houses on Okushiri completely destroyed by the waves
- 827 houses partially destroyed by the waves
- Total cost of tsunami: about US$600 million

Being prepared

Given the speed and power with which the 1993 tsunami hit the Hokkaido and Okushiri coastlines, it is surprising that more people were not killed. It seems that, in this event, community education greatly reduced the number of casualties. Many island residents knew the warning signs to look out for, so they started running away from the shore and towards high land as soon as they felt the ground judder from the earthquake. It is thought that a total of 1,200 people escaped the waves in this way, although the tsunami came so fast that many people were killed as they were running away.

Sea defences

Residents who survived could also be grateful for the 4.5-metre high sea defence walls that were built off the coast in the late 1980s. Even though some of these walls were destroyed by the waves, they did partly reduce the impact of the tsunami. Further sea defences have been built since the 1993 disaster. In fact, Okushiri is now known as the fortress island because 14 kilometres of its coastline are encircled by sea walls measuring 5-12 metres high. The other step the Japanese government is taking to protect people is to prevent them from living in danger zones. For example, on Okushiri there is now a memorial park where the entire village of Aonae was wiped out by the tsunami, and no new building is permitted in the area.

Wasted warnings

When seismometers recorded the Okushiri earthquake's size, the Japanese Meteorological Agency (JMA) sent out warning messages on television and radio channels in both Japanese and English. The warnings were issued after just five minutes, but unfortunately by then the first wave had already hit the island. In addition, not every home had a television or radio.

EYEWITNESS

❝ I'd like to tell people about the tsunami as long as I live... People should talk with their family members at least once a year to decide where to evacuate to. ❞

Kiyoji Hayashi, 57, fisherman

Improvements

Since the 1993 tsunami, all households on Okushiri Island have been equipped with radio receivers, and a new network of sensors has been installed which can set off alarms in all houses. There are four floodgates that can be closed to prevent waves from surging upriver. There are also 22 escape routes, all lit with solar-powered signboards, that residents can follow to get to higher ground. At the port, there is a huge platform raised 6 metres above the ground that port workers can escape to in the event of another tsunami.

Earthquakes and tsunamis are constantly monitored at the Japanese Meteorological Agency in Tokyo so that experts can warn people of danger.

PAPUA NEW GUINEA, 1998

The country of Papua New Guinea occupies the eastern half of the island of New Guinea in the south-west Pacific Ocean. Earthquakes are fairly common in this area, where the edge of one tectonic plate rests on the edge of another. On the evening of 17 July 1998, an earthquake 24 kilometres off the north coast of Papua New Guinea triggered a huge tsunami. The disaster wiped entire villages off the face of the land.

The tsunami hits

Many of the people living in communities along the Papua New Guinean coast felt the earthquake, which was strong enough in some places to make walking difficult and to knock things over. However, no tsunami warning was given because the quake was considered too small to create giant waves. The lack of warning proved to be fatal. Just over ten minutes after the earthquake, three speeding walls of water, each the width of the horizon, struck the Papua New Guinean shore. The waves measured about 4-5 kilometres from front to back and travelled across the shore at approximately 20 kph for about a minute.

The noise of the waves was so loud that it brought curious people out from their huts, whereupon they found the sea floor in front of them strangely empty of water. After the noise came a huge blast of air that blew people off their feet, followed immediately by the three killer waves. Debris found hanging high in trees when the water subsided gave evidence that the waves were up to 14 or 15 metres high – taller than a four-storey building.

TAKEN BY SURPRISE

The earthquake measured 7.1 on the Richter scale, so it was not large enough to trigger tsunamis on its own. Scientists have since concluded that the earthquake may have generated an undersea landslide. The sea floor off the north coast of Papua New Guinea drops into a steep trench, and the earthquake must have shaken sediments piled on top of the trench until they slipped and fell suddenly, causing a massive ripple in the ocean that created the tsunami waves.

Impact

The waves hit a 30-kilometre stretch of coastline, which is relatively narrow for a tsunami. However, unfortunately this was a part of the coast from which people could not escape. The water swept over a 300-metre wide spit, or strip of land, with the Bismark Sea on one side and the large, salty Sissano Lagoon on the other.

When the tsunami hit, villagers living on the spit had no way of escaping. Their route inland was blocked by the lagoon. The wave over-ran the flat, low-lying sand spit and washed people and their wooden homes into the lagoon. The villages of Arop and Warapu were totally destroyed. In other villages, palm and coconut trees were ripped up and houses were swept away. Many people were badly injured by debris. The waves washed people, most of them children, into the sea.

This is the spit of sand between the ocean (on the left) and the Sissano Lagoon (on the right) after the tsunami struck. The bare patches are where people's huts once stood.

Rescue efforts

The tsunami waves left many people with terrible injuries. Some villagers were wounded when they were swept across the lagoon and thrust into broken mangrove tree branches. Many victims were badly injured by debris. Rescuing survivors was not easy – for one thing, the tsunami happened at night-time when it was difficult to see where people were. Also, once the tsunami waves had receded, they left floods with water up to 10 metres high in places.

Helicopters and speedboats were sent to pick up injured people and take them to a hospital at nearby Aitape. The Papua New Guinea government did its best to get emergency supplies, food and shelter to the thousands of people who needed it, but the disaster area was very difficult to reach. A local airstrip was closed for a day or two after the tsunami struck, and for a while there was no road access to the devastated region. Additional help came from other countries, such as the USA, who sent sniffer dogs to help find survivors.

EYEWITNESS

❝ The patients are so badly infected now – the smell, the stench. They say you step off the plane there and you can smell the death in the air, but it's not only the death, it is infection. ❞

Jim Croucher, Catholic priest in the area

Sassano survivors search for belongings among the debris. Houses that weren't completely washed away lay in ruins, while stronger buildings, such as the religious school on the right, were swept in one piece off their foundations.

An important part of relief work after any natural disaster is helping the survivors to cope with their changed lives. This nun is comforting a woman and her baby who lost many relatives in the Papua New Guinea tsunami.

Difficulties and disease

The climate also made the situation harder to deal with. Survivors and the Papua New Guinea army had to begin burying bodies where they found them soon after the disaster, because the tropical heat was causing the corpses to rot quickly. Other rescuers went to sea in motorboats, towing nets to try to bring home floating bodies. Disease-carrying bacteria bred fast in the tropical conditions. At least 30 survivors lost injured limbs to gangrene, because bacteria-filled coral sand infected their wounds. And when barefoot survivors managed to carry their injured loved ones in their arms into small district hospitals, they found a distressing overflow of patients. Many people were left lying on the floor with multiple broken bones and cuts.

The lagoon was so contaminated by dead bodies that most of the fish and crabs in it died. The authorities closed off the lagoon to avoid the risk of decaying bodies spreading disease and death through the surviving population. In addition, the tsunami had washed alligators and other tropical wildlife into populated areas and these creatures had begun to feed on the dead bodies. Sadly this meant that it was difficult to find who was missing and many people were buried before being identified.

SURVIVAL STORY

One of the most amazing rescue stories of the Papua New Guinea tsunami was that of Apelis Munulai. This 32-year-old man was thought to be lost, but five weeks after the tsunami he was discovered adrift on the Pacific Ocean in a small dinghy. He had survived on nothing but rainwater.

Lessons learned

One reason that the death toll from the Papua New Guinea disaster was so high was that the waves struck with little or no warning. Many of the people who died were young children, who were too small or too weak to climb coconut trees or run out of reach of the tsunami's furiously powerful waves. The children were at home because it was the school holidays, rather than in their religious mission schools where they might have been saved by the stronger buildings.

Although people were devastated by the disaster, in the months that followed they began to look for ways to reduce the risk of such terrible loss of life in the future. Several thousand villagers decided that the only way to be safe was to keep away from the coast, so they rebuilt their homes further inland. But many people relied on the sea for their livelihood, so they could not move far away. Also, for less developed countries such as Papua New Guinea, building sea defences of the kind that help to protect Japan is not always practical or financially possible.

Sissano survivors and a member of the Australian army who helped in recovery efforts attend a ceremony of remembrance a year after the disaster.

CHANGING LAND

Tsunamis can alter landscapes. Sissano Lagoon was itself formed from water left behind after a tsunami that hit Papua New Guinea in 1907.

Preparation for the future

Before the 1998 disaster, few people on Papua New Guinea had been educated about tsunamis. Since then, tsunami preparation leaflets have been available to everyone and in schools children are being taught how to recognize tsunami warning signs and what to do if a tsunami happens. In the Papua New Guinea disaster there was no shaking of the ground to alert people of possible danger, but residents now know that if they hear a large roaring sound from the sea, especially at night when the ocean cannot be seen, they should get away from the coast as fast as possible. They are also told to watch out for the drawback effect, when the sea suddenly retreats from the shore just before the waves hit.

TSUNAMI COSTS

■ **2,200 people killed**

■ **1,000 people injured**

■ **5 villages totally destroyed**

Posters like this have a powerful message: if you ever spot signs of an approaching tsunami, drop anything unimportant and get yourself and other people to safety as fast as you can.

Evacuation platforms

Another cheap and practical solution that could help people to escape tsunamis on the coast of Papua New Guinea – and other similarly flat coastlines – is the provision of vertical evacuation platforms. These are large, sturdy towers with ladders that allow people to climb high enough to escape tsunami waves. The spit in front of the Sissano Lagoon was only 3 metres high at its highest points, so people had nowhere to climb to for safety. If high refuge platforms had been in place in 1998, many lives might have been saved.

DROP

PERU, 2001

In the middle of the afternoon on 23 June 2001, a massive earthquake measuring 8.4 on the Richter scale shook Peru. It occurred just off the coast of the country, when the South American tectonic plate moved up over the Nazca plate. People could feel the ground shaking right across southern Peru and as far away as northern Chile. The quake caused several landslides and damaged many towns and roads, killing around 120 people. It also triggered a serious tsunami wave train of four waves, the largest and most destructive of which was the third.

The tsunami hits

After significant rumblings from the earthquake, the next sign that a tsunami was coming was a sudden drawback of the ocean along a stretch of coastline in the region of Camana in south-western Peru. The sea was sucked up to 100 metres out from the shore for almost 15 minutes in places, during which time a few villagers were tempted to run out on to the exposed sea bed to pick up the fish that had been left behind. Then, just as suddenly as the sea had retreated, the first tsunami wave hit. This was the smallest. It was soon followed by three more waves, some of which were up to 7 or 8 metres high. These smacked into several locations on the coast and surged as far as 1.2 kilometres inland. Around 26 people were killed by the tsunami, which left a further 70 missing and presumed dead.

Far and wide

The tsunami was most destructive in Peru but was also seen in many coastal areas around the Pacific Ocean, including Chile, Hawaii and Japan. Tsunami waves arrived in New Zealand 16.5 hours after the earthquake, having travelled for 8,000 kilometres. By the time they hit the land these waves were only half a metre high, but they showed just how far and for how long tsunami waves can travel.

TSUNAMI COSTS

- About 96 people killed by the tsunami
- More than 200,000 people affected
- 2,000 buildings destroyed
- 1,000 buildings damaged

This low-lying coastal road was demolished by the waves.

The dashed line on this satellite image shows how far the tsunami waves moved inland at Camana.

Camana

EYEWITNESS

❝ All we heard were screams and then we saw people running, but many could not outrun the wave. ❞

Local resident, describing the moment when a tsunami wave hit the beach where he lived

Effects and aid efforts

The tsunami centred on the portion of coastline stretching from Atico town in the north of Peru to Matarani in the south. The area around the city of Camana was worst hit, with run-up waves up to 7 metres high. The tsunami destroyed 2,000 homes and other buildings and damaged a further 1,000, especially at the holiday resort of La Punta, south of Camana. In farming and fishing villages the houses were built from bamboo or adobe (mud), so were easily washed away. Even sturdy hotels, built from much tougher materials, were badly damaged. In some cases metal doors were bent in half from the sheer power of the water.

Farmland hit

The walls of water reached as high as the top of two-storey buildings in the village of La Quinta.

The Camana area was badly affected because the land along a 1-kilometre wide stretch of the coastline there is very flat. This plain was covered in bright green onion fields. Many of the people killed in this tsunami were workers in the onion fields who had been reluctant to leave their jobs before the end of the shift because they desperately needed the money.

As well as killing workers, the tsunami ripped out all the crops that the farmers had been growing. When tsunamis hit farmland like this, they often ruin it. The huge waves flooded 2,000 hectares of farmland with seawater, making the land salinated, or salty, and unsuitable for growing crops. In addition, the tsunami waves covered the land with sand, which clogged up the soil.

The mammoth task of rebuilding houses damaged by the Peruvian earthquake and tsunami could only begin once the debris had been removed.

Rescue and relief

The tsunami affected more than 200,000 people, thousands of whom were left without homes. They had nowhere to sleep or shelter in the cold winter air, where temperatures often dipped below freezing. Although there was a lot of wood from destroyed buildings, people were unable to build fires to warm themselves and cook food because the wood had been soaked by the tsunami.

Relief agencies, such as the Red Cross, sent supplies and workers to help. They provided water, food, blankets and tents, and medical care because many hospitals had been damaged by the earthquake. Relief agencies also supplied tools, such as shovels and wheelbarrows, to help people clear away the debris that had been scattered by the waves.

Reviewing the impact

The 2001 Peru tsunami made a huge impact on the land it hit and destroyed a large number of buildings. However, although any number of deaths is a great tragedy, fewer lives were lost in this tsunami than in previous ones. There were several reasons for this. The first was that most people in the area were familiar with tsunamis and knew that the drawback effect was a sign of danger, so they started to flee the area as soon as they saw the water retreat. The exceptions were some of the caretakers who had been brought in from elsewhere to look after summer houses or hotels until the tourist season resumed. Another reason was that the area had experienced tsunamis before, so some of the newer structures had been built with protection in mind. The Pan-American Highway, for example, was built on land high enough to avoid inundation.

Timing is everything

With this tsunami, timing was everything. The fact that the earthquake and tsunami occurred in winter actually saved lives. The beach towns of Camana are very popular with tourists. In summer, 5,000 extra people move here to work in the tourist industries while a huge number of holidaymakers come and go. If the disaster had happened during summer, the number of deaths and casualties would have been far greater. Also, the tsunami occurred in mid-afternoon when people could see the water drawback. And the tsunami coincided with one of the lowest tides of the year, which helped to limit the wave heights.

EYEWITNESS

❝ The animals and a vegetable garden were everything I had. I hoped to offer my children some education so that they could have a better life. But the sea has taken everything away. Only two pigs and a cow are left. The worst of it all is that our family is being pulled apart. My husband does not want to leave the rubble of our house. And I fear the sea will come over again. ❞

A 42-year-old mother of five who lived in a coastal community near Camana

Ongoing impacts

The economic impacts of the tsunami lasted a long time. The main industries in Camana are tourism and agriculture and the tsunami damaged both. In the long term people needed help rebuilding their homes. Water and sanitation supplies had to be mended or new supplies created, and farmers who had lost fields and fishermen who had lost boats needed help getting back to work. Farmers, for example, were supplied with tools and bags of fertilizer to help make their fields fertile once more, and fishermen were supplied with new nets.

These houses very near the sea were unaffected by the waves. The reason is that they are built on higher ground where the tsunami could not reach.

INDIAN OCEAN, 2004

The devastating waves of the tsunami that struck the Indian Ocean region on 26 December 2004 made it one of the worst natural disasters in history. The massive tsunami was caused by an underwater earthquake off the coast of Sumatra, an island in Indonesia. Some of the waves were up to 30 metres high – as tall as an eight-storey building. They destroyed entire villages and towns, killed more than 230,000 people and left more than a million others homeless.

KILLER QUAKE

The magnitude of the earthquake that triggered the Indian Ocean tsunami was underestimated at first, but many scientists believe it rated an incredible 9.3 on the Richter scale. The earthquake was caused by the slippage of about 1,000 kilometres of the boundary between the India and Burma tectonic plates off the west coast of northern Sumatra.

This remarkable satellite image shows seawater returning to the Indian Ocean just moments after the tsunami had struck Kalutara, Sri Lanka.

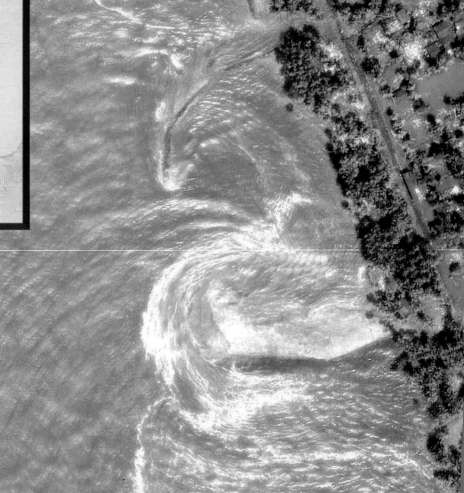

Fast and furious

The tsunami waves rippled across the open water faster than a Boeing 747 aeroplane. In seven hours they travelled as far as 5,000 kilometres to Africa, at which point they still had enough power to kill people and destroy property.

When the waves hit the shore at Sumatra, they sped across the land at up to 40 kph, travelling more than 4 kilometres inland. Then the waves retreated just as violently as they had come in, dragging out to sea anything they had picked up in their path. On the coastlines where the tsunami hit, a wave would be followed by a lull of 5-30 minutes. Then another giant wall of water would pound the land again, sometimes snatching away people who had returned to the beaches, thinking the crisis was over.

DISASTER DAYS

25 DECEMBER 2004
7.59 pm Earthquake begins in the Indian Ocean off north-west Sumatra, Indonesia.

8.15 pm Tsunami waves strike the coasts of northern Sumatra and the Andaman and Nicobar islands.

9.45 pm Tsunami waves hit Sri Lanka, India and Thailand.

11.21 pm A magnitude 7.1 aftershock occurs.

11.30 pm Tsunami waves reach the Maldive Islands.

26 DECEMBER
1.15 am Australia issues an alert to its western coasts.

3.00 am Tsunami waves hit Somalia, Africa.

5.36 am Small changes in sea level caused by the Indian Ocean tsunami are observed in the Pacific Ocean.

DECEMBER 2005
People are back at school and work, but many remain homeless and are living in temporary camps. Hospital staff are still helping orphans.

DECEMBER 2006
Most of the tourist area has been cleared; holidaymakers have begun to return to resorts. A third of the people made homeless remain so. Some aid organizations predict it will take four or more years for the region to recover.

Tsunami effects

The effects of the 2004 disaster were horrific. Along many coasts, the tsunami had turned a perfect, peaceful day of blue skies, sunshine and clear, calm seas into a living hell. People were drowned as the waves dragged them out to sea. Others were killed by heavy objects such as fridges and doors that were being tossed about violently by the waves. Friends, families and strangers tried to cling to each other in the dirt and the noise of the churning water, but were often dragged apart by its power. Most of the dead were local residents, but around 9,000 foreign tourists were also killed.

A battered family car is one of the few recognizable objects among the devastation on Sumatra after the Indian Ocean tsunami.

In Indonesia

The devastation caused by the tsunami varied from place to place. Indonesia suffered the worst losses with more than 130,000 people dead. The western end of the island of Sumatra, which was the closest inhabited area to the earthquake's epicentre, was totally destroyed. In places, up to three-quarters of the population of some coastal villages were killed. Fishing boats were wrecked and farmland was ruined.

In Sri Lanka

After Indonesia, Sri Lanka was the next worst hit. Over 31,000 people were killed, including 800 who died when the train they were travelling in was struck by a tsunami wave. More than 100,000 homes were damaged or destroyed. Around 400,000 people here lost their livelihoods when fishing boats, farmland and tourist hotels and resorts were wiped out.

Around the Indian Ocean

In other countries around the Indian Ocean, such as India, Thailand and the low-lying Maldive Islands, the terrible impact of the tsunami brought similar reports of death and destruction. Elsewhere, salty seawater contaminated many freshwater supplies, such as reservoirs and wells, and huge tracts of farmland. Roads, bridges and railway lines were wrecked or blocked. Trees and massive areas of plant life were uprooted and swallowed up by the sea. Overall, the damage to the physical environment was so vast that astronauts could see it from space.

Wildlife and habitats

On land, many animals escaped. Elephants, for example, ran for higher ground, which may confirm some people's belief that animals can sense the onset of earthquakes and other natural disasters. However, many marine animals had nowhere to go and were killed by the strong waves or died when they were tossed ashore and left high and dry. In Thailand, for example, the waves dropped dolphins 500 metres in from the shore and beaches were covered with dead fish.

RECORD-BREAKING DISASTER

With more than 230,000 people in over a dozen countries killed by this tsunami, it was the most destructive in recorded history. The second greatest loss of life from a tsunami was recorded in 1410 BC, when 100,000 people were killed by waves in Crete and Santorini in Ancient Greece.

Helpers return a dolphin to the ocean from a lake in Thailand where it was stranded after the tsunami.

INDIAN OCEAN, 2004

EYEWITNESS

❝ **There used to be towns and cities there. All the people once had homes, lives. Now there is nothing.** ❞

Scott Wickland, US Navy

Immediate assistance

As soon as news of the disaster became known, troops and volunteers from local regions and from abroad travelled to the stricken areas to help with rescue operations. Rescue efforts were made difficult because some of the badly affected regions were in remote places and roads, bridges, airfields, and jetties where boats could land, had been ruined by the waves. In some places the only way to reach survivors was by helicopter.

Aid and assistance

Within many of the affected countries, people gave all they could to help the victims of the disaster. In Sri Lanka, relief workers drove vans around to collect money, clothes, bottled water and bags of rice and lentils. Even in the poorest areas, people gave whatever they could.

This camp of temporary shelters, set up in Chennai, India for tsunami survivors, was flooded by heavy rains that could not drain into the waterlogged land.

38

Workers use the strength of trained elephants to help clear debris in Banda Aceh, Indonesia.

Around the world, governments pledged money and individuals donated cash and clothing to charities to provide assistance to the region. Worldwide charities and organizations such as the United Nations sent aid within days. They provided water purification units, food, shelter and tents, medical assistance, blankets, school supplies and sanitation equipment, but the problems with roads and other infrastructure made the distribution of aid tricky in some regions.

Clearing up

Many people were also involved in clearing up the dirt and debris amid the stench of rotting fish. Others concentrated on putting out fires or making gas lines and damaged electrical cables safe. In some places elephants were used to move and lift heavy wreckage to uncover victims and clear roads. In the days after the event, workers buried many of the dead people they found in a hurry because there was concern that the decaying bodies might spread disease.

FOREST SURVIVORS

Tribal peoples on Andaman Island, east of India, were thought to have been killed by the tsunami, until some started shooting arrows at helicopters that were flying over looking for survivors! It seems that stories about previous tsunamis must have passed down through the generations, so the islanders knew they should move deeper into the forests after they felt the first trembles of the earthquake.

CHANGING MAPS

The tsunami rearranged geographical features of the Indian Ocean – above and below the water. Some coastlines were completely reshaped, which means that one of the jobs for the future is to remake maps of the area!

A year after the tsunami, relief agencies such as Muslim Aid were in the process of building new houses in the Sumatran city of Banda Aceh, and other ruined Indian Ocean communities.

Longer-term aid

Rebuilding homes and lives after a disaster as terrible as the 2004 tsunami takes a very long time. Experts estimated it would be five to ten years before many places would be fully rebuilt. As well as the need to rebuild homes, the destroyed towns and villages needed new health clinics and schools, roads and important infrastructures such as water and sewage pipes. Many children whose parents had been killed by the tsunami needed care and somewhere to live, so new orphanages had to be built and responsible carers found. Another aspect of long-term assistance for victims was counselling. Many people became very depressed and distressed after the disaster and needed help to recover.

Rebuilding lives

In many places people had to rebuild their working lives, but this was made harder by the devastation the tsunami had left in its wake. In Indonesia, for example, the tsunami had swept 7 kilometres inland, spreading salt and mud over once fertile farmland. And in Sri Lanka, thousands of valuable rice, mango and banana plantations had been destroyed. Areas like this take years to recover and the effects on the economy can be immense. For the fishermen who had lost their boats, regaining a livelihood was slightly simpler. In India, fibreglass boats were donated to fishermen and some fishermen set themselves up as boat builders because the demand for new boats was so high.

The impact on tourism

In many of the countries hit by the tsunami, tourism had been a vital industry. However, holidaymakers were understandably frightened by what they saw on their television screens and most stayed away from the area after the disaster. Even resorts on the Pacific coast of Thailand, which were completely unaffected, were hit by cancellations. Thousands of people who worked in tourism, in hotels or restaurants or taking tourists on diving trips, lost their jobs. In Thailand the situation was so bad that the government began an advertising campaign to try to encourage visitors to return to the area.

The environment

The Indian Ocean tsunami also had a big environmental impact because it ruined wildlife habitats such as coral reefs and coastal wetlands. Some coral reefs were so badly damaged that they may be uninhabitable for many years. The fact that these reefs were important animal habitats is not only a loss for the world's wildlife. The reefs also brought tourists to the spot for diving trips, so their loss hits the local tourist economy as well.

This chunk of damaged coral from a reef off the island of Nicobar, India is evidence of some of the environmental damage caused by the tsunami.

TSUNAMI COSTS

- More than 230,000 people killed
- More than 1 million people made homeless
- 5 million people needing emergency relief
- Estimated cost of damage: US$9 billion

41

Making a difference

Some people argue that the loss of life in the 2004 tsunami was far greater than it should have been. One reason for this was the lack of warning. In the Pacific Ocean there are remote seismometers on the ocean floor, installed to detect and warn of tsunami-causing quakes. But there were no such sensors in the Indian Ocean. Therefore, even though the first waves to hit Thailand, Sri Lanka and many of the other areas did not arrive until two hours after the earthquake, people there were still taken by surprise. Some experts have stated that up to 40,000 people might have been saved if they had been warned.

EYEWITNESS

❝ Tilly said she'd just studied this at school – she talked about tectonic plates and an earthquake under the sea. She got more and more hysterical. In the end she was screaming at us to get off the beach. ❞

Mother of British schoolgirl Tilly Smith, whose family survived the tsunami

A lack of education

Tsunamis are rarer in the Indian Ocean, where there have been only seven in the last century, than in the Pacific. Therefore local people had not learned or been told what might happen after an undersea earthquake. One family of British tourists survived because their ten-year-old daughter remembered what she had been told about tsunamis in a geography lesson just weeks before flying to Thailand. Given that some tsunamis happen very quickly, often before warnings can be given, education can be a vital key to survival.

The need for safer buildings

When experts studied the damage to homes and hotels after the tsunami, it became clear that more people could have been saved if buildings had been better made. In many villages, religious buildings were the only structures remaining in the wreckage because they had been better built than any homes. Also, many people in reinforced concrete buildings, such as hotels, survived the tsunami if they were on the second floor or above when it hit.

Loss of natural protection

Many scientists believe the loss of life would have been less if human activity had not altered natural protection zones in the tsunami region. For example, many countries had destroyed coral reefs around their coasts to make room for shrimp farms or because the reefs got in the way of shipping. In places such as the Surin Islands off Thailand, coral reefs took some of the impact of the tsunami waves and saved the land. The removal of coastal mangrove trees and their deep tangled roots, to make room for buildings, may also have been a mistake as these could have helped to block the force of the tsunami.

Communities around the Indian Ocean are preparing for future disasters. These Indonesian children are practising how to evacuate to safety when tsunami waves are on their way.

Can tsunami disasters be prevented?

There have been records of tsunamis for thousands of years, and in the last 100 years tsunamis have killed almost 500,000 people. Tsunamis are forces of nature and as such they cannot be prevented. There will be more of these disasters and, with increasing numbers of people living by coasts around the world, there are likely to be more casualties in the future. Scientists cannot predict when a tsunami will happen, but they are working on ways of gathering information about undersea earthquakes more efficiently, so they can warn and evacuate people faster.

A tsunami warning buoy is installed off Indonesia in 2005.

Tsunami warning centres

Governments are placing more seismometers at the bottom of oceans. These measure the location, depth and strength of an earthquake and send the information to tsunami warning centres via satellites. If the data suggest a quake could create a tsunami, the centre sends out a warning. This may be an evacuation notice to regions nearby or a tsunami watch warning for areas further away, telling people to remain where they are but to listen to their radios for updates. Meanwhile, buoys on the ocean surface track the movement of unusual waves.

Since the Indian Ocean tsunami in 2004, more than 50 countries have begun to work together to link up tsunami warning centres and buoy networks and to share other Earth observations. This is called the Global Earth Observation System of Systems, or GEOSS. By combining information from around the world instantly, it should provide warnings of and responses to natural disasters more quickly than in the past.

SURVIVAL KIT

In some places people keep a tsunami survival kit ready, with items such as a torch, blankets, a first aid kit and water purification tablets packed in a bag that they can grab if they have to evacuate suddenly. Everyone in the family should know what to do and where to go if they fear a tsunami is on its way.

Computer modelling

Computers are also helping scientists to find ways of making people safer. Using the latest technology, experts can create three-dimensional computer models of the possible effects of a tsunami on different coastlines. They put in data, such as the shape of the coast and different wave heights, and information from previous events, such as the heights tsunami waves have reached, to work out how far tsunami waves are likely to run up a coast. This helps them to plan and signpost escape routes and to work out the height of land people need to reach before they can be safe.

Computers, such as this one being used at the National Disaster Warning Centre in Thailand in 2006, are important tools. They can help scientists to work out how tsunamis starting at different points in oceans will affect coastal communities.

SOME OF THE WORST TSUNAMIS IN RECENT HISTORY

1908, Italy 15-metre high waves killed 100,000 people.

1933, Japan Earthquake caused waves that killed 3,000 people.

1952, USSR Earthquake-driven tsunami killed 2,300 people.

1960, Chile Earthquake led to a tsunami with 10-metre high waves that killed 5,700 in Chile, 61 in Hawaii and 130 in Japan.

1976, Philippines Tsunami left 5,000 people dead.

1992, Nicaragua (see pages 10-15) 170 people died.

1992, Indonesia Earthquake triggered a tsunami that killed 1,700 people.

1993, Japan (see pages 16-21) 239 people died.

1998, Papua New Guinea (see pages 22-27) 2,200 people died.

1999, Turkey Earthquake claimed 17,000 lives and caused a devastating tsunami.

2001, Peru (see pages 28-33) 96 people died.

2004, Indian Ocean (see pages 34-43) More than 230,000 people died.

2006, Indonesia 2-metre high tsunami waves killed 300 people.

Glossary

aftershock Ground shaking caused by underground rocks repositioning after an earthquake.

asteroid A rocky object that orbits in space around the Sun.

bacteria Small, single-celled organisms, some of which can spread disease.

coral reef Rock-like structures built by small ocean animals called corals.

counselling A way of helping people to address their problems and work through their feelings.

crust The outer layer of the Earth.

debris Scattered material, such as tree branches or building rubble, that has been dislodged or broken and left behind after a tsunami or other disaster.

displacement When water is moved from one position to another.

earthquake Shaking of the ground caused by underground movement of rocks.

epicentre The point on the Earth's surface immediately above an earthquake.

evacuate To move away from a dangerous place to somewhere safe.

fertilizer A substance used to increase plant growth and productivity.

fjord A deep, steep-sided, U-shaped valley that is flooded with seawater.

foundations The underground structure that supports a building.

gangrene The decaying of a body part where the blood supply has been damaged by injury or disease.

habitat The natural home of a plant or animal.

headland An area of land that sticks out from the mainland and is surrounded by sea on three sides.

infrastructure Things built for services and communications, such as roads, telephone cables and water pipes.

inundation Flooding or swamping with water.

lagoon A shallow, saltwater pool or lake.

landslide The sudden movement of a mass of soil and rocks down a slope.

magnitude A measure of the size of an earthquake.

Richter scale A system used to measure and compare the strength of earthquakes.

sanitation The collection and treatment of waste water.

satellite A scientific object that revolves in space, usually carrying equipment that can transmit signals to and from Earth.

seismometer An instrument that detects earthquakes and measures their strength.

tectonic plates Giant sections of the Earth's crust that move slowly in relation to each other, giving rise to earthquakes, volcanoes and other natural hazards.

topography The shape of the land.

tropical Relating to the region of Earth on either side of the Equator that is warm and usually humid.

United Nations An international organization made up of representatives from many countries, whose stated aims are to promote peace, security and economic development.

volcano An opening in the Earth's surface through which molten rock, steam and ash may erupt, often forming mountains.

wave train A series of waves.

wetland Land that is constantly saturated (soaked) with water.

wharf A landing stage where boats can moor for loading and offloading.

Further Information

Books

Awesome Forces of Nature: Sweeping Tsunamis
Louise and Richard Spilsbury
Heinemann, 2003

Tsunami! (Nature's Fury series*)*
Anne Rooney
Franklin Watts, 2006

Tsunami Alert! (Disaster Alert! series*)*
Niki Walker
Crabtree Publishing Co., 2006

When Disaster Struck: Asian Tsunami 2004
John Townsend
Raintree, 2006

Websites

www.usgs.gov/search
Enter 'tsunami' into the search box for links to reports and information on tsunamis around the world.

www.geophys.washington.edu/tsunami
General information about tsunamis.

http://www.news.cornell.edu/releases/ July98/tsunamiVid.html A Quicktime movie of Liu's computer simulation model of the tsunami that struck Japan in July 1993.

http://walrus.wr.usgs.gov/tsunami/ PNGhome.html A US Geological Survey animation of the tsunami that struck Papua New Guinea in July 1998.

Index

Numbers in **bold** refer to illustrations.

Natural Disasters

Contents of titles in the series: